THE LOVER IN ME
HONORS THE LOVER IN YOU.

SAY THIS TO YOURSELF.
SAY THIS TO OTHERS.

LOVASTÉ.

-- ADRIAN MICHAEL

TITLES YOU MIGHT LIKE
BY
ADRIAN MICHAEL

--

loamexpressions

blinking cursor

notes of a denver native son

blackmagic

lovehues

notes from a gentle man

blooming hearts

Published by Creative Genius Publishing—
an imprint of A.Michael Ventures | Denver, CO
Cover art provided by Shutterstock.com

To contact the author visit adrianmichaelgreen.com

ISBN-13: 978-1523467525
ISBN-10: 1523467525

Printed in the United States of America

BLOOMING HEARTS

dear heart,

> you have been there.
> even when i didn't think i needed
> you. i am learning to yield more than
> defend. thank you.
> i don't say that enough.

dear heart,

> be gentle with my soul.
> it so wants to rush wildly
> with you & only you.

dear heart,

    i am no martyr.
    i suffer as you suffer.
    we became one
    the moment
    we spoke each other
    into existence.

dear heart,

keep trembling.
it tells me you're human.
that you feel the seasoning
poured onto your skin.
i ask that you grant me passage
inside your harbor.
you are my refuge.
my safety.
my anchor.

dear heart,

    we are the same breath;
    what we let out we let in.
    i can't remember
    what it was once like
    breathing on my own.

dear heart,

    look.
    i have seen magic firestorms,
    i've written you this before.
    but this one is grandeur.
    it's happening right now.
    there's a change in your weather,
    my body senses this.

dear heart,

    you see me.
    you understand
    and love on
    parts of me
    i have yet
    to claim.

dear heart,

if you are hurting and it was i that
did the hurting, come to me.
if it was another that caused you
sorrow, come to me.

dear heart,

    remind me to smile.
    keep it for me.
    in case i forget.

dear heart,

  we didn't invent love.
  we came across its vast body
  of water
  and plunged our bodies
  deep inside its belly.

dear heart,

> grant me access to your
> vault of secrets and i'll
> garage mine next to them;
> i don't want to keep
> anything from you.

dear heart,

    i have heard it all and seen it all
    before. show me who you are.
    ask me who i am.
    no one really took the time
    to water my soul.

dear heart,

do what makes you happy
and become the happiness
that you find.

dear heart,

hold my soul tight
when i just want to fall apart.

dear heart,

    i hear you.
    i can see why you
    think i come and go.
    it's no fault of my own.
    i'm a wanderer. traveling
    between worlds. falling for you
    in one and searching for you in the
    other.

dear heart,

　　all i want you to say is that i'm
　　always on your mind. that your
　　reign on my heart is forever. until
　　you utter these words, i am a bud
　　waiting to bloom.

dear heart,

whatever gives you peace. that's love.
whoever gives you peace. that's love.
wherever you give peace. that's love.
whenever you give peace. that's love.
however you give peace. that's love.

dear heart,

i can't tell you what you deserve
but go where your smile calls home.

dear heart,

> i can be a wreck and take it out on
> you. it is your sweet laughter that
> collects my dark words and kisses
> them into light.

dear heart,

> my soul smiles no matter
> how close or how far you are;
> thank you for being
> the lover that chose
> to love me.

dear heart,

what an honor it is
to wake up beside you.
you are my first and my last breath.
because of you i am full.

dear heart,

look in my eyes
& tell me i'm
beautiful.

loving speech
blossoms hearts.

dear heart,

    water me.
    even if
    the sun
    droughts
    your well.

dear heart,

the power you have
to give love fully
or take it all away
isn't what scares me.
i fear
that if i let you
feel again
i won't be able
to protect you.

dear heart,

> love me so that i may
> love you. heal me so
> that i may heal you.

dear heart,

you are enough.
i have always
known this.

dear heart,

how is your heart?
is it beating
how you want it to beat?
is there anything
i can say or do
to bring you joy?
may i toil
in your soil
and bring you
nutrients?
tell me what you need.

dear heart,

    i carry you
    with me
    wherever
    i go.
    and i see you
    on the tips
    of my fingers.
    each step
    i take
    brings me peace
    because i know
    i never leave home
    without you,
    dear heart.

dear heart,

    i look forward
    to watching you
    bloom,
    and bloom
    over and over
    again.

BLOOMING HEARTS

COOL RUNNINGS
IN DARK TUNNELS
a novel

BY ADRIAN MICHAEL
COMING SOON

Made in the USA
Monee, IL
18 July 2020